A souvenir guide

Beningbrough Hall and Gardens

North Yorkshire

National Trust

National Portrait Gallery

Breathing Life into Beningbrough

Beningbrough is not a place where time stands still. 'Living' history is constantly being created, whether in the historic gardens or in the groundbreaking interactive galleries.

Beningbrough's 18th-century house, garden and park came to the National Trust in June 1958 on the death of Lady Chesterfield. The hall echoed with emptiness, as most of the contents had been sold at auction. However the architecture of the building, including the superb woodcarving and dramatic entrance hall, means the house is remarkable in its own right.

Brought back to life

Over the years the gardens and parkland have been nurtured and a wonderful range of sights, scents, sounds and tastes have been cultivated – produce from the Walled Garden is even used in the Restaurant. The new Community Orchard and the beautiful Pear Arch in the gardens are particular treats.

The house is a treasure trove, with loans from the Ashmolean Museum, Oxford, a major bequest of period furniture from Lady Megaw, acquisitions such as the fantastic state bed and, as a result of an imaginative partnership, an important collection of portraits from the National Portrait Gallery, London.

Partnerships with the National Portrait Gallery

The National Trust has been in partnership with the National Portrait Gallery at Beningbrough Hall since 1979. The partnership is an important part of the Gallery's vibrant programme of collaborations, touring exhibitions and long-term loans, which make the national collection accessible to people all around the country. Beningbrough is an early Baroque mansion, so the partnership provides a unique opportunity to show important 18th-century portraits in appropriate historical surroundings.

In 2006, the Gallery and the Trust launched a major new initiative to refurbish, redisplay and enhance the visit to Beningbrough. *Making Faces* – Eighteenth Century Style brings the property's outstanding collection of 18th-century portraits to life in a series of groundbreaking interactive galleries in historic rooms that have been restored and fully opened to the public for the first time. A welcoming atmosphere, regular family events and range of exciting workshops made 2010 a very special year for Beningbrough, as it was proudly listed as a finalist in the *Guardian's* prestigious Family Friendly Museum of the Year Award.

Baroque basics
Baroque is a style of art and architecture which developed between the late 17th and early 18th centuries and originated in Italy. The key characteristics of Baroque architecture are extravagant and elaborate decoration, a sense of movement, bold projections, dramatic views and spatial drama. It is also common for Baroque buildings to have two evenly spaced floors, a basement and an attic level. On your way around Beningbrough Hall see if you can you spot any of these features.

Opposite The architecture of Beningbrough is as impressive today as it was originally intended to be

Left 18th-century portraiture and sculpture come to life in the interactive *Making Faces* galleries

Below Detail of a lion's head on an English mahogany commode, *c*.1740, typical of the fine craftsmanship to be seen at Beningbrough

The origins of Beningbrough

Mighty Beningbrough Hall rising out of the flood plain of the River Ouse has stood in this spot for nearly 300 years, the building itself being completed in around 1716. While the hall and gardens have their own intriguing story, the estate's history goes back well before their creation.

Our knowledge of Beningbrough, or 'Benniburg' as it was recorded in the Domesday Book of 1086, starts when it was owned by a man named Asford. The Forest of Galtres, over which the King had hunting rights, once surrounded Beningbrough and you can see references to the forest in the names of some of the nearby villages.

The monks of Beningbrough

In the 12th and 13th centuries much of the land which now forms Beningbrough passed to the Hospital of St Leonard, a religious foundation run by monks. The monks used large parts of the medieval park for arable farming.

In 1539, at the Dissolution of the Monasteries, St Leonard's Hospital and its lands were surrendered to King Henry VIII. Five years later, the land was sold to John Banester. Mr Banester's nephew was a man named Ralph Bourchier who inherited the land in 1556 at the age of 25. So began the long reign of the Bourchiers at Beningbrough.

The original house

The grand house which you see standing at Beningbrough today is actually the second hall to be built on the land (it might even be the third as it is possible that there was a monastic house on the estate before this). When Ralph Bourchier inherited the estate he set about building (or perhaps remodelling) a house on a site around 300 metres south-east of the present hall – a position south-east of the ha-ha in the parkland is the likely location of the hall.

Sadly, we don't have any images of the old house so we can only imagine what it might have looked like. However recent surveys suggest that it had a timber frame, and we know it had fine panelled interiors as some of these were reused in the present hall. The property was passed down a long line of Bourchiers and finally came to John Bourchier at the very beginning of the 18th century, when the face of the estate was to change forever.

Above The estate of Beningbrough – or 'Benniburg' – was recorded as early as the 11th century

Top right Ralph Bourchier

Opposite *Stag Hunting in Galtres Forest*, in the manner of Jan Wyck (1645–1700), in the Saloon. One of the few paintings from the Bourchiers' collection

Waste not, want not
This marquetery panel at the top of the Great Staircase has been recycled – it was originally part of the old Elizabethan hall. The initials 'RBE' stand for Ralph Bourchier and his first wife Elizabeth.

The owners of Beningbrough

In 1700, at the age of just 16, John Bourchier inherited Beningbrough. Four years later, he embarked on a Grand Tour of Europe. On his return, he set about building a brand new house with an innovative, continental design.

Young John Bourchier spent around two years in Italy, absorbing the Italianate Baroque architectural style and filling his head with fresh ideas and designs for a new house at Beningbrough. He returned to England and two years later married a wealthy heiress named Mary Bellwood.

Given John Bourchier's knowledge of Italian architecture, it seems likely that he played a major role in planning the hall. He would have been helped by the fact that many of the details he saw on Baroque buildings in Rome were published in architectural books available in England. Although the use of brick is an English tradition, much of the exterior detailing at Beningbrough is derived from Roman sources. The paired cornice brackets just below the roof, the vertical strips of stone marking the corners and projections of the façades, and the curious window frame above the entrance door with its curved ears are all details taken from Italian Baroque buildings.

Above The vaulted corridors of the first floor that run the entire length of the house

Left *John Bourchier the Younger*, by John Vanderbank, 1732 – a later John Bourchier who lived at Beninbrough in the mid-18th century

Right Top of a pilaster showing the detail and craftsmanship found throughout Beningbrough

Architecture on a grand scale

Very little is known about the actual construction of Beningbrough Hall, although the building probably took five or six years to complete. Yorkshire was a great regional centre for craftsmanship in the 18th century, and we do know that William Thornton, a talented wood carver from York who also worked at Castle Howard, Bramham Park and Wentworth Castle, supervised the construction of the hall.

The Earles

It was Margaret Bourchier, the last of the Bourchier line who held the house for the longest, for over 65 years. She married Giles Earle in 1761 and around eight years later they left the comfort of Beningbrough with their young son, William, to explore the wonders of France and Italy. Beningbrough Hall was shut up, waiting patiently for its owners to return. It was only some years later that the family took up residence once again at the hall.

Sadly, the Earles' two sons died fighting in the war against Napoleon and so the Bourchiers' hold on Beningbrough slipped away in 1827 when Margaret Earle died. She left the estate to the Reverend William Henry Dawnay, a close friend of one of her sons.

Airs and graces
Much to the amusement of others, Margaret Earle (above, by Sir William Beechey [private collection]) returned from France with a newfound sense of fashion and wonderfully obscure accent. In a letter to her brother, Mrs Theresa Parker of Saltram wrote that Mrs Earle was 'dressed very French' and was speaking in 'as broken English as if she had never seen England for more than two months'.

The Dawnays

Below Lieutenant-Colonel
Lewis Dawnay who
inherited Beningbrough in
1891, his wife Victoria and
their four young children

Between 1827 and 1916 the Beningbrough estate was owned by the Dawnay family. William Henry Dawnay inherited Beningbrough from Margaret Earle when he was 55 and he and his wife, Lydia, made the hall their home.

It was probably William Henry who knocked down the wall between two ground floor rooms of the house to make a large drawing room, used for entertaining.

New generations of Dawnays inherited, but it was not until 1891 that the house and gardens reverberated to the sounds of a young family. It became the home of Lieutenant-Colonel Lewis Payn Dawnay, his wife, Victoria and their four children. During this time substantial improvements were made, including the installation of electricity.

The family enjoyed skating on the pond in the winter, cricket weeks in summer, putting on theatrical performances in the Great Hall, even 'tobogganing' down the main staircase on tea trays!

Grand house going cheap

In 1910, at the age of 32, Major-General Guy Dawnay inherited Beningbrough. He was an officer in the Army but left to become a merchant banker, being recalled to the Army at the outbreak of war in 1914. In June 1916 the decision was made to sell Beningbrough as Guy needed to be near London for business once the war had ended.

The estate was sold in November 1916 to a Cambridgeshire farmer called William Abel Towler for £137,000; a low price caused by the agricultural depression. Towler split the 6,100-acre estate into parcels of land including one parcel of 375 acres (the hall, Home Farm and park) which Lady Chesterfield bought for the very low sum of £15,000. She and her husband took possession of the house in July 1917.

'A series of private theatricals was given at Beningbrough Hall on January 5th, 6th and 7th. On Wednesday Colonel and Lady Victoria Dawnay kindly invited the school children of Newton and Shipton. All the performers acted with spirit and ability.'

The Easingwold Advertiser,
15 January 1898

Above **Guy Dawnay**

Left **The Great Hall**
in 1906, when a gallery
connected the first-floor
corridors

Lady Chesterfield

Enid Edith Wilson, a wealthy shipping heiress, became Lady Chesterfield following her marriage to Edwyn Francis Scudamore-Stanhope, 10th Earl of Chesterfield, in 1900.

There was quite an age gap between the couple, Lord Chesterfield being more than twice as old as his young wife, who had a reputation for being rather demanding. They lived at Holme Lacy in Herefordshire until 1909, when they sold the property and moved to London. They remained there until 1917 when they finally came to Beningbrough.

The Chesterfields furnished Beningbrough lavishly with beautiful furniture and pictures from Holme Lacy. They completely redecorated, perhaps with help from the leading country house decorators of the day – Lenygon and Morant.

'I never had a hunting lady before, I nearly packed it in, then she seemed a bit kinder and I settled down and mastered her frantic ways.'

Miss Constance Seabrook,
Lady Chesterfield's maid

Right *Enid, Countess of Chesterfield*
(1878–1957), by Ellis Roberts, 1900

Called into service

Left Graffiti left by L. Godson in 1939, one of the servicemen who stayed at Beningbrough during the Second World War

Below This Model 232 telephone is believed to have been situated in the Great Hall with at least one other extension below stairs where the SNCO or Duty NCO in charge of the domestic staff had an office

Lord Chesterfield died in 1933 and in 1941 Lady Chesterfield temporarily moved from Beningbrough Hall to Home Farm, making way for servicemen from nearby RAF Linton-on-Ouse. The finest furniture and pictures were safely stored away, not to be unpacked until after the war in 1947 when Lady Chesterfield finally returned to her luxurious home. She remained at the hall until her death in November 1957, aged 79. Although she had wanted to keep Beningbrough in the family, she had known this was impossible – there would be death duties to pay and, in the post-war period, she didn't have enough assets to cover these. Beningbrough was instead offered to the Treasury and later, in June 1958, came to the National Trust.

Billetted at Beningbrough

In 1941, following a raid on Germany, British bombers were trailed all the way to the airfield at RAF Linton-on-Ouse, just two and a half miles away from Beningbrough. The disastrous events that followed led to a new chapter in the Beningbrough story.

RAF Linton-on-Ouse was hit hard by a barrage of German bombs with deadly consequences; amongst the dead was the RAF Station Commander. So it was decided that the RAF SNCO (Senior Non-Commissioned Officer) aircrews should be moved to a safer location. Beningbrough Hall became living quarters and a mess, whilst Lady Chesterfield moved to Home Farm. In the summer of 1943 an overseas squadron of the Royal Canadian Air Force (RCAF) also took up residence at Beningbrough.

The top two floors of the hall provided sleeping quarters for the men, while the ground floor was used as a dining room, ante-room and bar. We can only wonder what it was like for the RAF and RCAF servicemen who, against a backdrop of wartime desolation, found something of a safe haven, a retreat, at Beningbrough Hall. Sergeant Clifford Hill, a gunner in one of the seven-man crews of the Halifax Bombers (and pictured here), recalls his first glimpse of the hall:

SPEECH ON THIS TELEPHONE IS NOT SECURE

BENINGBROUGH HALL 334

FOR DIALLING INFORMATION SEE DIRECTORY

'It was a cold winter's day as we drove from Linton-on-Ouse along the country lanes and through the grounds, catching our first sight of the Hall which was to be our home for the next five months. I have vivid memories of the place. We piled out of the truck and dumped our kit on the ground outside the main entrance and gazed up at the magnificent façade.'

A Journey through Beningbrough

'John Bourchier had the vision to plant an Italian palace in Yorkshire – a fascinating property with so many stories to tell!'

Laurence Wright, house volunteer

of bricks and slates salvaged from decayed outhouses, as well as the oak wood flooring which was originally in the Great Hall.

The approach

As you walk towards the house, passing under the Clock Tower, you soon come to the north front of the property. In traditional Baroque fashion, the building's face includes a strong projecting middle section. Italian features include Doric capitals, which top the pillars either side of the front door. These are quite plain and angular, giving this side of the house a strong, masculine presence. The curly-topped Ionic capitals of the pillars at the south front of the house give a much softer, more feminine impression.

To the left of the Clock Tower is a cobbled yard with some railings in the corner. These are the newly restored kennels. While Lady Chesterfield loved her horses, his Lordship loved his Labradors and one of the Beningbrough breed even won at Crufts.

On your way up the steps to the large front door, it would be easy to miss the mysterious iron lever by the bushes. This was connected to a cable which ran under the turning circle and would have been pulled by servants to open the grand gates, impressing visitors as they arrived at the hall.

Above This lever would remotely open the grand gates to visitors

Left The lettering on the sundial was re-painted following the discovery of old photographs

Opposite The north front of Beningbrough Hall

The Stable Block

Walking into the yard, surrounded by the late 18th-century Stable Block, you might feel you have stepped back in time. The building here has been sensitively converted, preserving the exterior and the main structural interior elements. Where once horses and grooms had a home, you can now find the reception, shop and learning areas.

Time certainly does not stand still at Beningbrough, as testified to by the Latin inscription over the sundial. When the Trust acquired Beningbrough, the wording had faded over time. The words 'TEMPUS EDAX' (meaning 'time is voracious') were discovered in an old photograph and were re-painted.

Just a short walk from the Stable Block, opposite the walled garden, you will find the Restaurant, the only entirely new building constructed during the Trust's restoration programme in the late 1970s. It makes use

Lady Chesterfield's love

In the early 1920s, Lady Chesterfield set up a stud farm at Beningbrough, first breeding hunting horses and then racehorses. One of her finest moments must have been leading in her horse, Sun Castle, pictured here shortly after winning the St Leger in 1941.

The Great Hall

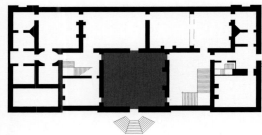

The Great Hall, a double-height space with imposing fluted pilasters, provides a sense of almost overwhelming splendour. With a striking resemblance to the classical grandeur of Baroque palaces in Rome, this room must certainly have been shaped by John Bourchier's experiences in Italy.

The Great Hall would have been an awe-inspiring entrance. It connects a lot of the ground floor rooms and was designed to impress as well as to serve as a busy circulating space. Its grandeur is now accentuated by the series of monumental portraits of several generations of 18th-century British monarchs which come from the National Portrait Gallery's collection.

A touch of colour

When National Trust conservators stripped back paint on the plinths supporting the pilasters, they discovered that they were made from solid York stone. This was used as the key for the creamy white colour in which the pilasters were redecorated. At the same time, the Trust re-laid the floor as it had originally been, with smooth flagstones.

In the 18th century this space would have been bustling with servants going about their duties; this is why there is so little furniture in this area and the decoration is so hard-wearing.

Left The Great Hall

Sculpting faces

Sculpted portraits, like the bust of Pope Clement XIV above the fireplace, often decorated the entrance halls of Roman villas, the ultimate inspiration for Baroque houses like Beningbrough. This impressive piece was carved in Rome in 1771 by the Irish sculptor, Christopher Hewetson. It was bought by former owners of Beningbrough, the Earles, as a memento of their time in Rome in 1770–71, when Mrs Earle became pregnant and Pope Clement gave her special permission to stay in a convent.

Casual versus formal

These portraits show three generations of the same family. King George I and II are presented in traditional poses and their crowns and extravagant robes symbolise their power rather than their personality. Frederick's portrait is much more relaxed. Unlike his father and grandfather, he adopts an informal pose breaking with tradition and suggesting his interests as an art lover.

Straight laced

Look closely at the feet of the nobleman in this portrait, which is one of the National Portrait Gallery's loans. You'll see his shoes are tied with lace. It is because of this practice that today we have 'shoe laces'. The nobleman is William Russell, 1st Duke of Bedford, by Sir Godfrey Kneller, *c.*1692.

Left The bust of Pope Clement XIV in its commanding position above the fireplace

The Great Staircase Hall

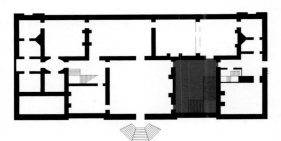

As if by magic, the staircase appears to hang unsupported in the air. The secret to the trick lies in ingenious architectural craftsmanship; each wooden stair conceals a long bar of iron which pushes far into the wall, acting as a cantilever for a person's weight as they use the staircase.

This area provides a link between the Great Hall and the original state apartment (now the Drawing Room) on the ground floor and the Saloon on the first floor, where large parties and formal dinners were held. It would have been reserved exclusively for the owners and their guests, who would have climbed it in formal procession on special occasions.

Illusions at Beningbrough
John Bourchier found a number of ways to cut costs, while producing impressive illusions of grandeur. For example, the intricate fretwork of the banister at first glance could be mistaken for delicate wrought-iron work. Remarkably, the spindles are in fact carved in wood, probably by William Thornton, Beningbrough's chief craftsman and master woodworker.

Servants' staircase
Just to the left of the Great Staircase is a small door which opens onto another tiny set of stairs which run alongside their much grander counterpart. This was a working staircase, used by the servants who would not have been permitted to use the Great Staircase.

Left The intricate fretwork of the banister is not wrought in iron but is in fact carved in wood

Above The servants' staircase

Wealth, taste and power

This view of Beningbrough was painted by J. Bouttats & J. Chapman in 1751 for John Bourchier the Younger, who had inherited the estate from his father in 1736. Bourchier proudly hung this picture over the chimneypiece in the library at Micklegate House, the new residence he had started building in York after his appointment as High Sheriff in 1749. Such paintings tend to represent the owners' wealth, taste and power and this painting certainly does just that. However, it possibly exaggerates the property by including two wings and a full turning circle which may never have existed. Alternatively, it is possible that these features were built but torn down – maybe in the late 18th century when the Stable Block was built. If you look carefully at the top of the hall in the painting you will see four impressive statues greeting visitors. These were not an artist's elaboration – there are indeed four sockets on the stone plinth here, so it is likely that these figures did once stand proudly atop the house.

Fine furniture

The English mahogany commode beneath the stairs was created in around 1740 and may be the work of James Richards. He was the principal carver for the royal barge made for Frederick, Prince of Wales, whose portrait hangs in the Great Hall.

Left The Staircase Hall

The Blue Bedroom

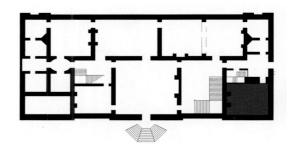

Although dressed as a bedroom, this space was used by the Dawnay family in the 1890s as a billiards room and may originally have been the common parlour – an everyday living and dining room. It was probably never a bedroom but now serves as the perfect setting to showcase a magnificent blue state bed.

The Conservatory

Adjoining the Blue Bedroom is the late 19th-century Conservatory which was built for the Dawnay family by Richardsons of Darlington. It is now a relaxing space where you can sit, read and enjoy the variety of plants around the room. If you look out of the windows you will see the area below where the old kitchens once stood. Sadly these burned down some time ago, however the outlines of the rooms and doorways can still be seen.

The bed in this room was probably made for Holme Lacy in Herefordshire, where Lord and Lady Chesterfield once lived but was sold when the Chesterfields moved to Beningbrough in 1917. Though John Bourchier was a wealthy Yorkshire gentleman, he would not have been able to afford a bed like this – they could cost more than the rest of the contents of the house put together and could only have been purchased by the richest of aristocratic families. It's not surprising that they were so expensive, given the rich velvet, damask and silk material that was used to finish them and the intricate trimmings which would have been painstakingly made by hand.

Left The blue state bed was acquired in 1980 with the generous help of the Art Fund (then the National Art Collections Fund)

Opposite The Dressing Room, finely furnished with the types of luxury items it might once have contained

The Closet and Dressing Room

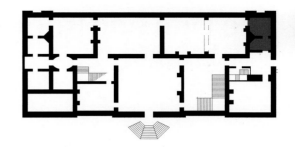

The four main bedchambers at Beningbrough are on the south side of the house and are served by small dressing rooms and closets, or 'cabinet' rooms, at the corners.

These two rooms would originally have formed the south-west state apartment that was made up of four rooms. The State Apartment was reserved for the Bourchiers' most honoured guests and contained the owner's most precious possessions. Bedrooms were much more public spaces than they are today and it was common for guests to be entertained in them. These ideas of access and privacy derived from royal palaces where access to the monarch was carefully controlled.

Closets like these would have also been used as bathrooms, with chamber pots concealed in cupboards – this is where the term 'water closet' comes from.

Mysterious marks
The strange marks on the panelling at the end of the Closet are cigarette burns left by RAF and RCAF servicemen who were billetted at Beningbrough during the war. The Dressing Room was used as a bar during this time, and a counter for payment was installed in the Closet, which has left scratches on the door frame.

The Drawing Room

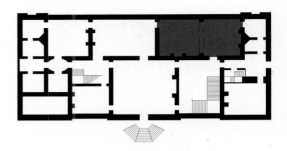

Look around the top of the walls here and you might notice something unusual: the carved patterning is different on the two sides of the room. This is because the Drawing Room was originally two separate spaces – a bedroom and a withdrawing room that formed part of a state apartment, used by important visitors.

It was probably during the 1830s that the Dawnay family, who previously owned the house, removed the wall dividing the two rooms. By this time, the fashion for ground floor bedrooms had passed and there was a greater need for large reception rooms on this floor.

Below The Drawing Room

Wonderful woodwork

The magnificent woodcarving in this room reflects the importance of what was once the former State Bedchamber and Withdrawing Room, displaying the talents of William Thornton and his team of craftsmen who worked at Beningbrough. The beautiful frieze in the former State Bedchamber features intricate patterning and the initials 'JMB', which stand for John and Mary Bourchier, for whom the house was originally built.

Not as they appear

The panelling and woodcarvings in the room are not in their original positions – they were moved around and jumbled up during 19th century alterations and again after 1917, when Lady Chesterfield moved in and had the woodwork stripped of paint to reveal the pine beneath.

Some of the portraits here were, until recently, thought to be original features, depicting members of the Bourchier family. When they were taken down for conservation, old labels on the backs showed that they had in fact been bought by the Dawnays in the 1890s and were nothing to do with the Bourchiers.

Costume made

You might notice the peculiarly shaped arms of the chairs with red covers in this room. They were cut away like this to allow ladies to sit down in their dresses, which were extravagantly large in the 18th century.

Above The fine details of the carved-wood frieze include shells, vases and palm fronds

The travelling Sandwich

Too busy to leave his desk, or possibly the gambling table, the Earl of Sandwich (1st Lord of the Admiralty in 1776–77) asked for some meat to be placed between two pieces of bread and brought to him; it was named the 'sandwich' after the Earl. This portrait painted in 1740 by Joseph Highmore celebrates his Grand Tour between 1737 and 1739, traditionally to Italy and Greece, but which took the Earl even further afield. The exotic fur-lined costume was often worn by westerners while travelling in the East, and in the background of the portrait are the dome and minarets of Haghia Sophia in Istanbul. If you look closely at the paper on his desk, you might be able to make out another wonder of the world – a pyramid.

The Dining Room

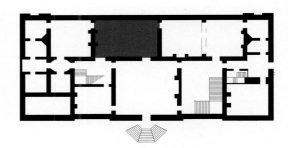

Coming in from the cold and sitting down to a hot meal in this room must have been quite an experience. Despite its distance from the kitchens, the Dining Room (or the 'Great Parlour' as it would probably have been called until the mid-18th century) was probably Beningbrough's main dining room by the 19th century.

The walls of this room are of panelled wood, rather than hung with fabric which would have absorbed the smell of food. Though painted a pale green colour, the room would originally have been decorated a stony white. The National Trust chose the current scheme as an ideal colour to complement the gold-framed portraits on the walls. The colouring was inspired by a scheme found at another Baroque house, Boughton, in Northamptonshire.

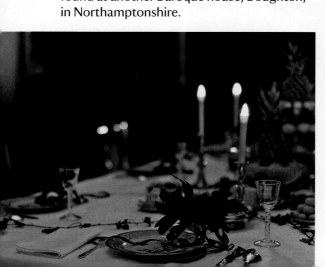

All askew

The double doors leading out to the gardens may look somewhat strange crammed into the corner of this room. The problem is that the rooms either side of the Dining Room are not of equal length, meaning that this room is positioned slightly off centre. The doors needed to be situated at the corner of the room, so that from the outside they form a dramatic entrance in the very middle of the house.

Above The Dining Room

Left The table laid for a festive occasion

Jacob Tonson the Younger

Richard Lumley, 2nd Earl of Scarbrough

John Tidcomb

The Kit-Cat Club

In the 17th century a new political party emerged. Whig politicians and their supporters shared a commitment to uphold the 'Glorious Revolution' of 1688 (the overthrow of the Catholic King James II) and the Protestant succession to the English throne. In the 1680s, leading Whig politicians and their followers founded the Kit-Cat Club, the most distinguished and influential club of its day. The group (men only) met regularly in a London tavern, and was apparently quite riotous, despite its public reputation for culture and politeness. A bar bill for a single day's drinking in 1689 ran to '20 gallons of claret, 6 of canary ... 4 of white wine'. The club took its name from the mutton pies that were served up by the owner of the tavern, Christopher Cat.

It was the Duke of Somerset who began the custom of presenting a portrait to the club's secretary, the publisher Jacob Tonson (his son Jacob Tonson the Younger [top left] became a Kit-Cat member). In the first two decades of the 18th century, Sir Godfrey Kneller, artist and member of the Kit-Cat Club, painted nearly 40 club portraits. He even created a brand new 'kit-cat' portrait size which was larger than a standard portrait, making the images almost life-size. This new format also allowed Kneller to include one of his sitter's hands therefore ensuring that, although these club portraits seem uniform, no pose is exactly repeated and every man retains his individuality. Nearly half of Kneller's Kit-Cat portraits are on display at Beningbrough, while the remainder can be seen at the National Portrait Gallery, in London.

'Hence did th'Assembly's Title first arise, And Kit Cat Wits sprung from Kit-Cats Pyes'

The Kit-Cats, A Poem, anon (1708)

Charles Montagu, 1st Duke of Manchester

Charles Mohun, 4th Baron Mohun

Algernon Capel, 2nd Earl of Essex

The State Apartment

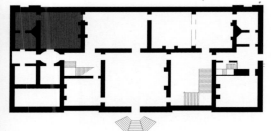

Traditionally, the more powerful an individual, the further into an apartment they would be allowed. John Bourchier applied this principle at Beningbrough, creating a grand guest apartment comprised of a withdrawing room, bedchamber, dressing room and closet.

As the form of the original state apartment was lost with the creation of the current Drawing Room, the National Trust has re-created the State Apartment here, in the intact south-east apartment.

The State Bedchamber

The state bedchamber was the most richly decorated of the state apartment rooms in the English Baroque house and the focus of such rooms would have been the state bed. This bed was probably made in the early 18th century and was brought to Beningbrough in around 1917 by Lord and Lady Chesterfield when they moved to the estate. It was bought by the National Trust after Lady Chesterfield's death in 1957, when the contents of the house were sold. These beds were such an important feature that bedrooms would frequently be decorated around them, as here where the shape of the window pelmets matches the cornice of the bed. They were also symbolic, showing the wealth and status of the owner.

Left The second of the great
state beds at Beningbrough

The State Dressing Room and Closet

These intimate rooms would have been reserved for use by the occupant of the State Bedchamber and only close friends would have been invited to enter. In the winter, when the larger rooms in the house would have been bitingly cold, the owners and their guests would have retreated to these smaller rooms to keep warm – enjoying the heat from corner fireplaces.

Kings would have met with their key ministers and advisors in their own closets, which were also known as 'cabinet rooms'. This is the origin of the political word 'cabinet'.

Portraits for all

The pine-panelled walls of this room display an impressive series of mezzotint engravings. Mezzotint engraving was invented in the 17th century and is a print-making technique which uses light and shade rather than line. The ability to reproduce pictures in this manner revolutionised the art world – making portraits of well-known figures such as these politicians and aristocrats widely available at comparatively affordable prices. The mezzotints in this room are copies of the Kit-Cat Club portraits in the Dining Room.

The richly carved Closet would have been used for washing (the cupboard held a chamber pot). Again, only important guests and friends would have been allowed into such private rooms, often to conduct business which they wouldn't want overheard.

Only half the picture

This portrait of James Brydges, 1st Duke of Chandos, by Herman van der Myn, c.1725, is quite unusual. Look closely at the bottom right hand corner of the picture and you will see a toe as well as the edge of an artist's easel. The portrait was once larger but was chopped in half some time ago. We know from 18th-century descriptions that if we were to find the other half, we would see the toe's owner, the Duke's wife, who was depicted painting his portrait.

The stepped chimneypieces were specifically designed for the display of ceramics. Oriental porcelain was very fashionable from the late 17th century and similar chimneypieces were introduced by Queen Mary at Hampton Court. We have been able to recreate this effect with loans from the Ashmolean and Victoria and Albert museums.

The Saloon

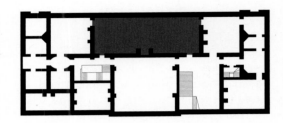

John Bourchier would probably have called this room the 'Great Dining Room'. It would have been used for large parties, county balls, family celebrations and banquets; bustling with life and energy.

To allow room for celebrations, this space would have been kept uncluttered, with chairs pushed to the edges of the room, just as it is now. Georgian ladies would have paraded through the Saloon, showing off all their finery. The spirit of the room is kept alive today through events such as fashion shows.

At first glance, you might think the elaborate Italianate decoration of the room is moulded in plaster. In fact the detail is another example of master craftsman William Thornton's skilful woodcarving. And to further confound the appearance of great luxury, these panelled walls were in fact used to conceal all manner of construction waste, the equivalent of hiding the sweepings under the rug!

'Fame is sweeter than a white rose'
The Taylor children in this portrait offer white roses to each other, reflecting their family motto – 'Fame is sweeter than a white rose'. The boy in the left of the picture, being crowned with a laurel wreath by his two sisters, is Brook Taylor who would become a famous mathematician. Brook holds a recorder which is a symbol of family harmony. The artist was John Closterman, *c.*1696.

Ongoing conservation
The two early 18th-century mirrors hanging on the wall are from Holme Lacy where Lord and Lady Chesterfield once lived. Conservation work at Beningbrough is ongoing and these two mirrors were carefully cleaned and treated in 2009 to prevent their deterioration.

Above The spirit of the room is kept alive through events such as 18th-century fashion shows and dancing at Christmas

Left The 18th-century mirrors that hang in the Saloon were conserved in 2009

Opposite The Saloon

Lady Chesterfield's Rooms

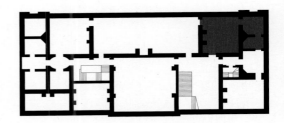

The next three rooms together form the third of Beningbrough's apartments.

Lady Chesterfield's Bedroom

Lady Chesterfield used this as her bedroom from 1917. In fact, it has always been a bedroom. The bed, with its tufted canopy is the third of the Holme Lacy beds now at Beningbrough and, although more modest than the beds on the ground floor, it is a beautiful example of elaborate upholstery.

A volatile actress

The unusual sick-bed portrait on the wall next to the bed is of Margaret Woffington, the celebrated Irish actress who was affectionately known as 'Peg'. She was notorious for her bitter rivalries with other actresses, even stabbing one in a performance, as well as for her supposed love affair with Britain's leading actor, David Garrick. The painting is unusual in that it shows her after she collapsed and became paralysed in 1757.

Lady Chesterfield's Dressing Room

This Dressing Room is laid out in the same way as the Dressing Room directly below it on the ground floor, with panelling and a corner fireplace providing shelves for the display of china.

Left The third of the great State Beds at Beningbrough

Fascination for fireworks

Look above the fireplace in Lady Chesterfield's Bedroom. Can you find the pot showing two boys pointing to a small block on the floor? The object is actually a firework. The colourful explosives were invented by the Chinese and, fascinated by these newly introduced curiosities, the British imported great quantities. The detail of this china pot reflects that fascination. Frederick, Prince of Wales, whose portrait hangs in the Great Hall, was known for his firework parties in London.

Lady Chesterfield's Bathroom

Lady Chesterfield transformed this closet into a luxurious modern bathroom in the 1920s. The taps can be shut away in their own cupboards to create a more finished look to the room, a very extravagant touch. When billeted at Beningbrough during the war, the RAF and RCAF servicemen thought it a real treat to have a dip in the sunken bath, which was a very modern feature when it was built.

On your way out

The Reading Room is a place to rest, read, write and relax, but its original function is a mystery. It might have been an upstairs dining room – the marble bowl now in Lady Chesterfield's Bathroom may be an original 18th-century feature which once lived in the niche in the lobby outside this room. It may have been used by guests for washing hands or by servants for washing wine glasses. On leaving the Reading Room, the view down the Great Hall Staircase is very impressive. This panel on the staircase displays the initials of John and Mary Bourchier, who built Beningbrough, and the date 1716, the year of its completion.

Top Lady Chesterfield's Bathroom

Making Faces – Eighteenth Century Style

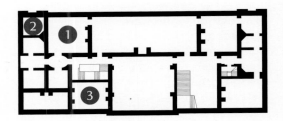

These galleries combine the National Portrait Gallery's 18th-century collections with low- and high-tech interactives to let you explore sitters' and artists' parts in creating the portraits.

These interactive galleries bring Beningbrough's outstanding collection of 18th-century portraits to life. They are the result of collaboration between the National Trust and the National Portrait Gallery, supported by the Heritage Lottery Fund.

1 Visiting Portraits

In this gallery the National Trust and the National Portrait Gallery collaborate to put on temporary displays based around 'visiting portraits' from the National Portrait Gallery's collection in London.

2 Portrait Explorer

Next door you will find 'Portrait Explorer', an IT study-room where you can use touch-screen computers to search the entire National Portrait Gallery collection.

Below *The Shudi Family*, by Marcus Tuscher, *c*.1742

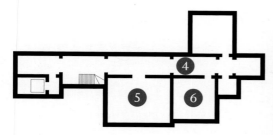

3 Family Matters

Here you can experience an introduction to historic portraiture through a series of activities based around three family portraits. In the decades after a major economic crash in 1720, many British people became wealthier and, just like the very richest individuals, they too wanted portraits of themselves. So entrepreneurial artists began to paint 'conversation pieces', like that commissioned by the Shudi family. In this gallery you can find out how 18th-century portraits like these give clues to their subjects' identity and status through pose and expression, costume and props, composition and background.

4 Portraits Tell Stories

One example of a portrait telling a story is that of Anna Maria Jenkins (above right). The bindweed flower she holds represents her beauty while the dog, wearing a collar engraved 'Jenkins', symbolises loyalty – she was hoping to find an eligible husband.

5 Getting the Picture

Here you can explore sitters' and artists' different roles in commissioning and producing portraits in the 18th century. The 'Virtual Portrait' computer lets you commission your own 18th-century-style portrait, which is then displayed alongside all the other historic portraits and can even be emailed home.

6 Turning Heads

Find out more about the making, meaning and significance of 18th-century portrait busts in a variety of materials. Here you can have a go at modelling a portrait and get up close and personal with a number of sculptures (like this one of James Cook) which you can handle to get a better idea of how they were created.

Above *Anna Maria and Thomas Jenkins*, by Angelica Kauffmann, 1790

Right Marble bust of James Cook, by Lucien Le Vieux, 1790

Below Stairs

Mystery cellar
This is one of the cupboards in the large 'keeping cellar'. This area was also a male space but we don't know exactly what it was used for. Maybe it was a storage area or perhaps somewhere for the servants to clean and polish pots and pans.

A staircase descends from the ground floor, each step worn down with hundreds of years of footsteps. The extravagance of the house fades into much gloomier surroundings. Despite the dark appearance, the below stairs area of the house was once alive with servants going busily about their duties.

As was usual, this basement area was split into areas for men's work and areas for women's work. The butler's bedroom/workroom is at the men's end of the corridor, as is the wine cellar. The butler's main job was to manage the household and supervise the servants. One of his most important jobs would have been looking after the beer and wine.

At the top end of the passageway are the women's rooms. There is a china store and also the housekeeper's room, next to which was her bedroom. The housekeeper's main role was to look after the house and its contents. She would have supervised preparation of tea, including sandwiches, cakes and jams.

Left The butler's job included keeping a close eye on supplies of alcohol...

Above ...while the housekeeper would oversee the preparation of tea trays

The Victorian Laundry

This building is separated into Wet and Dry Rooms, as it was in Victorian times. A laundry maid's day was a long one: if she lived in Newton village she would probably have woken at 4am to walk to work.

Wet Room

A laundry maid would probably have used the large bowl at the back of the room to boil clothes and the smaller one for general washing – these would have been heated from below by fires. The dolly, the wooden device that looks a bit like a four- or six-legged stool, would have been twisted strenuously through clothes in soapy water, forcing out the dirt, while clothes which were very stained would have been scrubbed vigorously against a washing board. It would have been exhausting work and they weren't expected only to do Beningbrough's dirty washing. It was once a common belief that washing dried in country air was healthier than that dried in a town, so the family would have sent their laundry up to Beningbrough from their London and Brighton houses.

Dry Room

The laundry maid would bring the wet clothes in here to be dried, starting by passing them through the rollers of the iron-framed mangle to squeeze out the water. This would also be used for pressing dry clothes. The big box mangle in the centre of the room was used to press large damp sheets or tablecloths while the bumpy rollers of the goffering machine would have been used to finish the pretty frills on the edges of sheets.

Above Sinks in the Wet Room

Right A selection of washboards

The Parkland and Gardens

From the 12th and 13th centuries, when monks farmed here, to the early 18th century, when John Bourchier built the Baroque hall surrounded with formal gardens and avenues of lime trees, the estate grounds have always been intriguing.

Counting the number of rings within a tree trunk is a useful method for dating trees. This technique has been used to discover that most of the trees in the park were planted between 1830 and 1870. At this time, Thomas Foster was the Head Gardener at Beningbrough. He was responsible for over 300 acres of parkland, as well as the gardens, and it is likely that the landscape surrounding Beningbrough is largely down to him.

Later owners all left their own marks on the landscape. In particular, Lewis Payn Dawnay, who inherited in 1891, planted 11,000 trees, extended the lawn to the south of the house, created two ice-skating ponds and replanted the north avenue with broadleaved lime trees (since replaced with common lime trees).

An artistic intent

William Sawrey Gilpin (1762–1843) was an accomplished artist and watercolourist, specialising in landscape. Discharged from service as third drawing master at the Royal Military College in Marlow, Buckinghamshire (later relocated to Sandhurst) at the end of the Napoleonic Wars, he turned to landscape gardening, drawing on his artistic skills and his 'painter's eye'.

In 1827 he was hired by the Dawnay family to advise on the landscaping of the parkland at Beningbrough. His method of working was generally to produce rough sketches and notes, which explained in detail his ideas for different areas of the landscape. We are fortunate that these written documents have survived at Beningbrough. His influence on many areas of the parkland was extensive and is still apparent today, although some of his suggestions, such as a low wall near the South Lawn, intended to provide a formal architectural break between the park and the pleasure grounds, appear not to have been implemented.

Pressed for purpose

The Dawnays also established a real sporting culture at Beningbrough, making good use of the cricket pitch, croquet lawn, and tennis and squash courts. People would even pay special visits to use these facilities.

When the Chesterfields purchased the house, home farm and park in 1917, Lady Chesterfield converted buildings into a horse surgery. Though the Chesterfields didn't make many changes to the landscape, they were keen gardeners, restoring the two small formal gardens by the south front of the house and taking particular pride in the South Border, which was always at its best when visitors came to stay during the St Leger meeting each September.

During the Second World War ornamental gardening virtually stopped and the South

Lawn was ploughed up to grow cabbages and potatoes. When the National Trust accepted Beningbrough in 1958, the gardens were in a fairly rundown state. The Walled Garden was rented out to a market gardener and for the next 20 years the Trust made few changes to the garden.

Living, changing gardens

When restoration of Beningbrough began in 1977, the gardens were in much need of attention. The National Trust redesigned the two small formal gardens; the Walled Garden, which had by then come back under Trust management, was sown with grass and the walls planted with climbers; and an area of derelict glasshouses and service sheds was removed to make way for the new Restaurant and Italian-style sunken lawn. The gardens have continued to develop with a range of new planting schemes. They are constantly growing, changing and surprising us with different sights, scents and sounds.

Top The park in 1916

Above Most of the trees in Beningbrough's parkland date to the landscaping of the 19th century

Opposite Beningbrough Hall in its landscape

The gardens

Overlooked by the Victorian Conservatory and close to the Victorian laundry yard, the planting here is influenced and inspired by that era and represents what might have been grown when the Dawnays lived at Beningbrough in the late 19th century.

The West Formal Garden

This small garden by the south front of the house has a 'hot' theme. Sizzling colours are used to give the space a warm atmosphere, which you can enjoy as you walk around the lovely beds or rest on one of the benches.

The East Formal Garden

This enclosed garden has a 'cool' theme to complement the 'hot' feel of the West Formal Garden just a few paces away. Muted white and blue colours create a calm, tranquil space; the perfect place to take some time to sit and relax. The trickling water in the formal pond and the sweet scent of white mock-orange (*Philadelphus*) in the early summer are just part of the sensory experience to be enjoyed here.

The South Lawn

This large grassy area to the back of the house provides stunning views of the surrounding parkland and is the ideal space for a picnic. Just in front of the house are two large 'knots' (the Bourchier family symbol) filled with gravel. These were installed in 2008 to celebrate the 50th anniversary of Beningbrough coming into the care of the National Trust and provide a link between the East and West Formal Gardens. The stone-filled design was inspired by a Samuel Buck sketch of around 1720 which shows how the gardens might have looked and includes patterns in-filled with coloured gravel.

In September 1898 the Duke of Cambridge planted a variegated oak – you can't miss it as it is directly in the centre of a path. A sapling propagated from this oak tree was planted in January 1995 to commemorate the National Trust's centenary.

Below These knots were created in 2008 to celebrate the 50th anniversary of Beningbrough coming into the care of the National Trust

Gardening tip
If you have very dry soil, try cistus shrubs.
They do well in hot sunny weather, can live
in sandy soil and come out in beautiful
five-petal flowers. They do particularly well
here in the Italian Border.

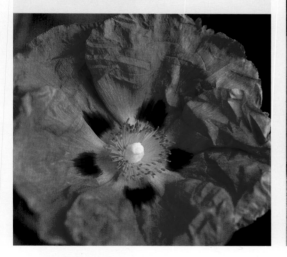

The Italian Border

This border has also been called the main
border but was replanted between 2009 and
2010 taking inspiration from John Bourchier's
travels in Italy. The plants used are not
necessarily Italian, but they have been chosen
because they would thrive in the hot, dry
Mediterranean climate. Among the exciting
new additions are the Italian cypress and the
trachycarpus palms.

The Double Border

From April until October, this more formal
border is alive with an array of beautiful plants,
though it is designed to be colourful
throughout the year. As you stroll down the
border you might catch the scent of citrus
from the mock-orange plants, which are also
found in the East Formal Garden, and the
sweet smell of the shrub roses. The climbers
on the walls, such as clematis, are particularly
striking in spring and summer.

Above The Italian Border
was recently replanted and
reflects John Bourchier's
Italian interests

Left A sketch of 1719–23,
by the printmaker and
engraver Samuel Buck,
shows how the gardens
might have looked to the
south of the house in the
early 18th century

The Walled Garden

The National Trust restored the Walled Garden in 1995, recreating the original paths and planting over 120 fruit trees.

Amongst those planted were varieties known to have been grown in the York area in the early 19th century. One of the most famous varieties is the Ribston Pippin, which was very popular with the Victorians and was first grown at Ribston Hall near Knaresborough. It is good for cooking, eating raw and for making cider.

Above The Walled Garden today

Right The Walled Garden in 1916

Hot beds

Against the north wall of the Walled Garden are some wooden-framed boxes with sloping glass lids. These are called cold frames and they are used to extend the season for growing vegetables like lettuce, spring onion and radish. A layer of manure is placed at the bottom of the frame to provide warmth and nutrients for the vegetables, and a layer of soil is added to this for the roots to grow into. Lantern cloches, looking like tiny greenhouses, provide a similar function. The Victorians used manure on the beds to grow vegetables earlier in the season, even managing to grow melons.

Victorian ingenuity

To help control the eventual size of trees, gardeners today use what is called 'rootstock'. A bud from a fruit variety that is known to grow to a certain size is grafted onto the rootstock of another. The resulting fruit tree's growth will then be limited to the desired size. Recently, Beningbrough's gardeners were digging in the Walled Garden and found huge stone slabs laid two to three feet under the surface. The Victorians had used them to block root growth, achieving a similar result to that achieved through the use of rootstock.

Further ingenuity can be seen in the peculiar arched holes in the walls around the Walled Garden. These are what remain of the 17 chimneys that ran through the bricks here. Fires lit at the bases of these chimneys would produce hot smoke and heat the air in the flues inside the walls. The warmed bricks would protect the grapes, peaches, nectarines, apricots and flowers that grew up the walls from biting frost.

Centre Some of the produce of the Walled Garden

Right Remains of the Victorian chimneys that warmed the brick walls, protecting tender plants from frost

The Kettles
Cyril Kettle (below left) was the head gardener at Beningbrough in the post-war period and proudly stands by Beningbrough's cold frames. His wife May (below right) was the housekeeper at this time and can be seen with their children under the Pear Arch, which still survives today.

A space for all

Beningbrough Hall and Gardens is a place for everyone and local community groups and artists are encouraged to get involved with the property.

A community garden

Just beyond the Walled Garden is the Community Orchard, where each tree is cared for by a local family or community group who visit Beningbrough to look after it. There are also a number of 'Artrageous' spaces around Beningbrough's grounds – for example, the apple sculpture in the orchard which also gives shelter to all sorts of crawling wildlife.

The American Garden

Just around the corner from the Community Orchard is the American Garden. This area has a wild and natural feel about it and on a sunny day the space is beautifully dappled by light shining through the branches of the large trees found here. There is even a little nature pond which is perfect for spotting wildlife.

In the 19th century many plants were brought to Britain from North America, as it was considered very fashionable to display these novel varieties in gardens. Beningbrough's American Garden is one of the few remaining gardens of this type. The name can be a bit misleading, as sometimes gardens like this contain very few plants which are actually of American origin. For example, plants originating in the Far East were also termed 'American' because of their novelty. American

The Beningbrough Tea Party
The teapot sculpture was created by a local blacksmith and students and instructors from Henshaws Art and Craft Centre in Knaresborough. It was inspired by the blue and white ceramics collection from the Ashmolean Museum in the house.

Above The apple sculpture forms the centrepiece of the Community Orchard

plants generally need a lot of moisture and are lime-hating – any plants which fitted these criteria, wherever they originated, were planted in American Gardens.

The original plants after which the American Garden was probably named have sadly not survived – they did not do well in Beningbrough's lime-rich soil. Over the years, plants more suited to the conditions were introduced but by the mid-1970s the area had become very rundown. It was an untidy mass of elder, sycamore and bramble, which local children delighted at playing in. The area was regenerated around this time and the overgrowth was cut back. The garden was given a new lease of life, opened up and the once shady space became much brighter. Now, in general, trees, plants and shrubs which are suited to limey soil and need little moisture are planted here and these are mainly of North American origin.

Memorial trees

A number of commemorative trees have been planted in the American Garden. Two maple trees were placed here by Canadians to commemorate the airmen of the Royal Canadian Air Force who were billeted at Beningbrough during the Second World War. An English oak was also planted here by RAF servicemen on the 50th anniversary of their colleagues being shot down over Europe.

Three of the towering silver birches tell the story of a British Army officer who had been stationed in Berlin at the end of the Second World War. He married a German lady whose German husband had died fighting the Russians. She showed him a picture of her first husband's grave, which was marked only by two birch twigs. The British officer planted two silver birches at Beningbrough in memory of his wife and her German husband and some years later a third was planted for him.

Below Cherries growing in the American Garden

Seasonal Beningbrough

Beningbrough's grounds have something to offer in every season, from the beautiful scents of the Walled Garden and Cherry Tree Lawn in spring and summer, to a winter's walk through the American Gardens or across the parkland on a snowy afternoon.

Spring and summer

As the bulbs around the gardens start to spring into life, marking the end of the chillier months, the sweet scents of the new season waft through the air. Brightly coloured tulips start to appear, while a yellow carpet of daffodils provides a warm welcome in the American Garden. The trees on the Cherry Tree Lawn are full of pink blossom ready to spread around the garden. Salads are already growing in the cold frames, ready for an early harvest. The purple alliums and geraniums in the South Border opposite the Orchard set the colourful scene for this area. In early summer a sea of bluebells floods the park, especially around the Pike Ponds as you exit the estate, and by late summer buddlejas, fuchsias and dahlias are in full swing, providing a brilliant show of reds and purples.

Left **Tulips in April**

Right **Maple leaves dappling autumn sunshine in the American Garden**

Wildlife at Beningbrough

Beningbrough's grounds are teeming with wildlife. There are too many different species to list, but be sure to watch out for butterflies which are especially attracted to the buddlejas in the Walled Garden and the Double Border.

The American Gardens are home to bats, such as the tiny pipistrelle which comes out at dusk to feast on insects – as many as 3,000 insects in one night. If you are very lucky you might catch a glimpse of the tawny owl that sometimes visits the American Garden, or the kingfishers, sand martins, heron and otters along the riverbank in the parkland. The banks of the River Ouse are also the only place where you will find the bulbous green tansy beetle, which feeds on the tansy plant. Out in the parkland dead oaks are deliberately left to provide food and shelter for beetles and other invertebrate. Also look out for rabbits, squirrels and wild roe deer in the park.

Autumn and winter

The trees and shrubs in the parkland are not to be missed in the autumn – around September and October time the vibrant reds and oranges of the plants are stunning. The flat land provides the perfect place to watch the autumn sun setting over the beautiful scenery.

The wintry frost and snow settled on the branches of the trees and other plants across Beningbrough's grounds can really make a Christmas walk special, while the wetter months often bring flooding of the river. This creates a seasonal lake and the view of this from the Double Border can be breathtaking.

Above A walk in winter sees Beningbrough in a new light

Beningbrough Today

Beningbrough has a long history but its spirit is still very much in the present. The atmosphere is friendly and welcoming and people of all ages are encouraged to explore, learn and enjoy.

Beningbrough is a wonderful setting to take a trip through history, learning all the ins and outs of 18th-century portraiture, while regular events, 'Artrageous' workshops, community activities and a strong learning programme for schools really do bring the past bursting into the present.

A varied and constantly changing programme of events, supported by people passionate about what the National Trust seeks to preserve, ensures that the history of Beningbrough is kept alive